FRISBEE® disc BASICS

FRISBEE® disc BASICS

by Dan Roddick

Illustrated by
Bill Gow

Photographs by
James Morse and Jack Roddick

Created and Produced by
Arvid Knudsen

Prentice Hall, Inc.
Englewood Cliffs, New Jersey

Dedicated to:

The children in all of us, with the hope that we will let them go outside and play.

Special thanks to Carmen Brown, Jennifer Cahow, Steve Cahow, Maria Teresa Diaz, Ruben Hector Diaz, Liesl Grannell, Heidi Hartert, Scarlet Kruger and Nathan Schultz for serving as models for our photographs. And special thanks, too, to Jo Cahow for gathering all the young people together.

Copyright © 1980 by Dan Roddick and Arvid Knudsen

Illustrations and Photographs copyright © 1980 by Arvid Knudsen

All rights reserved. No part of this book may be reproduced in any form or by any means, except for the inclusion of brief quotations in a review, without permission in writing from the publisher.

Book Design by Arvid Knudsen

Printed in the United States of America

Prentice-Hall International, Inc., London
Prentice-Hall of Australia, Pty. Ltd., North Sydney
Prentice-Hall of Canada, Ltd., Toronto
Prentice-Hall of India Private Ltd., New Delhi
Prentice-Hall of Japan, Inc., Tokyo
Prentice-Hall of Southeast Asia Pte. Ltd., Singapore
Whitehall Books Limited, Wellington, New Zealand

10 9 8 7 6 5 4 3 2 1

Library of Congress Cataloging in Publication Data

Roddick, Dan, 1948-
   Frisbee basics.

   SUMMARY: Introduces techniques and strategy for using Wham-O's Frisbee with emphasis on form.
   1. Flying discs (Game)—Juvenile literature.
[1. Flying discs (Game)] I. Title
GV1097.F7R62   796.2   80-10194
ISBN 0-13-331322-0

ORIENT HEIGHTS
3-20-81

The use of the trademark FRISBEE and other trademarks using the word FRISBEE in this book is with the permission of and under license from Wham-O Mfg. Co., 835 E. El Monte St., San Gabriel, California. FRISBEE is a registered trademark of Wham-O Mfg. Co., U.S. Trademark Reg. No. 679,186 issued, May 26, 1959, for toy flying saucers for toss games. References in the title and text of this book to FRISBEE and FRISBEE discs and saucers are intended to be and are limited solely to the disc products manufactured and sold by Wham-O Mfg. Co., under the trademarks FRISBEE, SUPER PRO FRISBEE, MINI FRISBEE, FASTBACK FRISBEE, PRO MODEL FRISBEE.

CONTENTS

- **AN INVITATION** 6
1. **A LITTLE FLYING DISC HISTORY** 8
   - It Flies
2. **LET'S PLAY** 12
   - But First, warm up!
   - What to wear
3. **THROWING** 15
   - The Cross Body Backhand
   - The Forehand
   - The Overhand
   - After It Leaves Your Hand
   - Practicing
4. **CATCHING** 23
5. **FLIGHT PLAY** 29
   - Tipping
6. **FUN AND GAMES** 35
7. **PICKING THE RIGHT DISC** 44
8. **WHAT'S HAPPENING?** 46
   - **INDEX** 48

AN INVITATION

Some things, like some people, seem to be immediately likeable. The Frisbee disc is definitely one of those things. It's always fun to see somebody's first try at throwing. They usually fidget around with the grip, plant their feet and give it a heave that immediately turns over and rolls away—but they *laugh!* It felt good in their hand and they were tempted by the challenge. They tried so hard to do something that looked so easy.

First catches are great too. The disc glides and floats; they run and grab, but it spins out of their hand and flies away, tempting again.

Although the basic mysteries of disc play are fun,

the purpose of this book is to introduce you to the satisfaction of controlling those mysteries. If you are like most kids, you already have one or two out in the garage, in the closet or on the roof. And you've probably already tried to throw and catch a little—so perhaps this is more of a reintroduction and an invitation to the fun of the Frisbee disc.

You will be given all the basic tools that are needed to have a lifetime of fun with the Frisbee disc. You'll learn how to make it spin and curve, hover and float, or even come flying back to your hand. You'll discover that the "catch" in this game is not a catch at all but more of a dance with the flight. You'll learn the games we play now and how to make up the ones we haven't thought of yet. There's plenty of room for you in the game—come on—let's play!

1

A LITTLE FLYING DISC HISTORY

People have been throwing disc-like things for a long time. Almost certainly, kids are responsible for the very early developments because they seem to have the ability to have fun with almost anything. Adults need equipment to play their games, but kids take what they have and make the game. Flat wood chips were probably the first "sailors" with paper and metal pie plates a later, popular scaling item. It was the plastic age, however, that brought the idea of disc play to large numbers of people.

The man behind the Frisbee disc we know today is Fred Morrison. In the late 1950's he began to experiment with the new plastic materials for these toys, shaped like miniature flying saucers. His first few experiments were not successful because the discs were much too hard and brittle. Eventually, however, he found materials that were firm enough for good flight and yet soft enough for safety and durability.

Fred and his wife sold the new toys at county fairs in Southern California and they were quite a sensation. The people were amazed at the straight, accurate flights of Morrison's "Flyin' Saucer." In fact, Fred would often encourage sales of his disc by promising to sell the invisible wire that the disc flew on for one dollar with the disc thrown in for free!

Morrison soon sold his idea to Wham-O Mfg. Co. who dubbed the product "Frisbee" and marketed it nationally. The result was an initial fad and the beginning of Wham-O's development of the product. They now offer 15 models of Frisbee discs, and over 50 other companies produce other flying discs. Now each year, more discs are sold than baseballs, basketballs and footballs combined. That's a lot of invisible wire!

It Flies

The invisible string seemed reasonable to the folks watching Fred Morrison's new toy because the disc actually does *fly*. When you throw a ball, you really only give it a long drop. It produces no lift to counteract the pull of gravity.

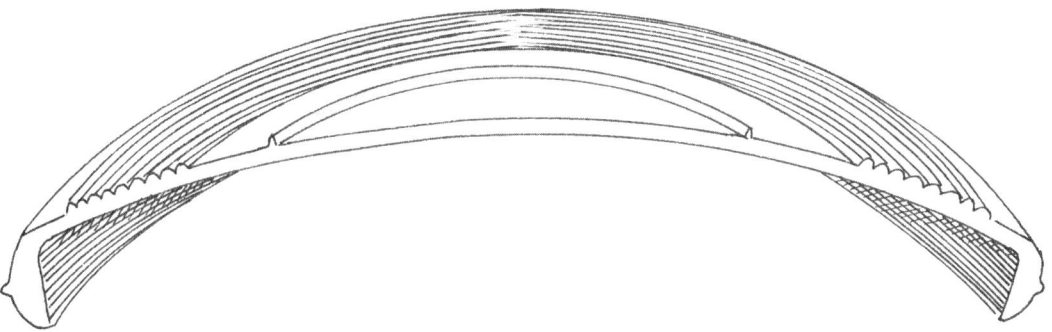

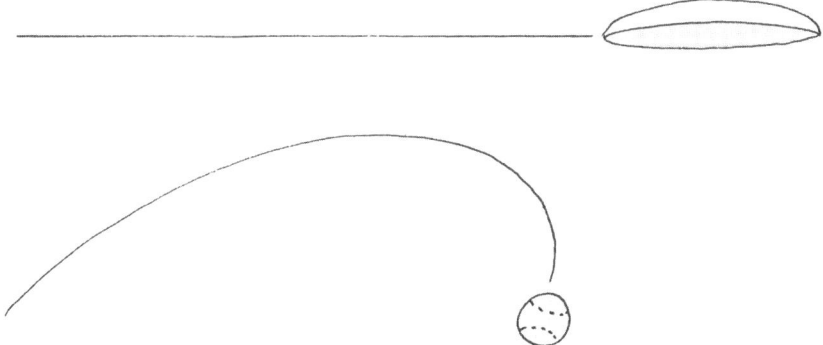

The flying disc, however, is like a little aircraft. As you throw it, you give the all-important SPIN. Spin is what makes it happen for a flying disc. Without spin the disc flutters lifelessly and falls. The rotation gives both the potential for LIFT and STABILITY. In the same way that a toy top almost magically balances itself when spinning, a disc gains gyroscopic sta-

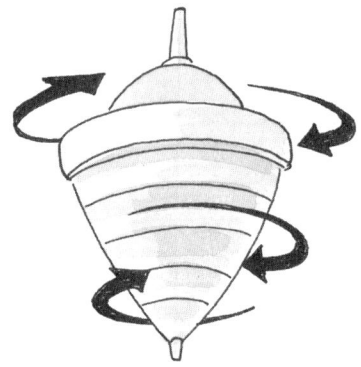

bility from its rotation. The stable disc then serves as a small wing or airfoil while in flight. The action of the air passing over the disc is almost identical to that around an airplane wing.

Of course, your throw also produces AIR SPEED and the air moves more rapidly over the rounded, upper surface producing a relatively lower pressure area which results in lift.

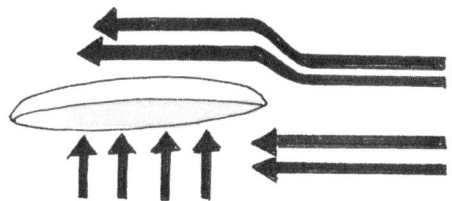

Also like an airplane, the flight of the flying disc is related to its position in the air flow. If it is banked to the left, it curves left. A right bank produces a curve to the right. If the leading edge or nose is up, the disc will rise and stall. Nose down produces a dipping descent.

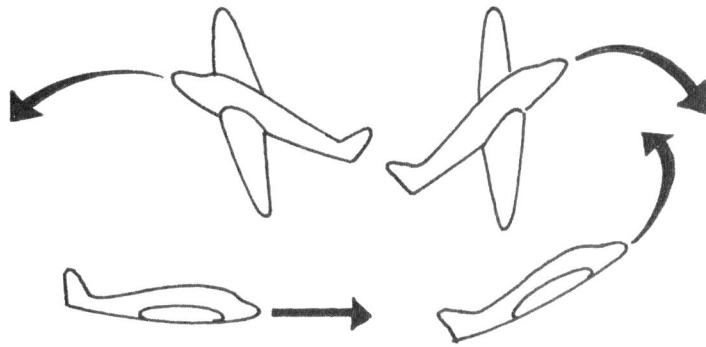

There is a big difference between a plane and a flying disc however. You have to set all the controls for the flight before you take off. Once it leaves your hand, it's on its own. Now we'll show you the controls.

2

LET'S PLAY

But First, Warm Up

Flying disc play can be very physically demanding so it is wise to always warm up your body before going full speed. Trying a difficult leaping catch or a very fast throw before your muscles are ready can result in uncomfortable strains and possible injuries. Try some of these exercises that have been developed specifically for disc play.

No matter what disc activity you will be doing, it is best to begin slowly using the exercises followed by some jogging and then light throwing at short range. This not only gets your body ready, but also prepares you mentally.

#1 DEEP BREATHING
As you move slowly from position 1 to 4, slowly inhale with your lungs full when you are upright and empty when you touch your toes. Move slowly and do 5 cycles. Relax.

#2 ARM STRETCH
Clasp your fingers together and lock your wrists. Do five sets in both the raised and lowered positions flexing both your shoulders and wrists. Gradually stretch farther on each set of movements.

#3 ELBOW ROTATION
Make large circles with your elbows. Rotate first in one direction, then reverse. Keep your palms flat on your back and flex fully. Do ten circles in each direction.

#4 FULL BODY ROTATION
Begin with a moderate swinging motion and build to a full, flexing turn involving your head, torso, hips and legs. Twenty swings should do it.

What to Wear

It's most important to be able to move freely. Many players wear loose shorts and T-shirts or no shirts. Footwear is a matter of taste but cleated shoes are usually worn for Guts, Ultimate and the field events. Flat-soled athletic shoes are most popular for freestyle as they allow for spinning and sliding.

3

THROWING

There are a *lot* of ways to throw a Frisbee disc. Just listing the variations would fill most of these pages. We will show you four of the basic throws here to get you started.

The Cross-Body Backhand

The Grip

There really are very few *musts* in disc play. Almost everyone has a slightly different grip, but you must develop a method that provides a firm hold on the disc. How firm? Well, imagine you are holding a canary. Hold tightly enough to keep him from escaping but not hard enough to kill him. Most beginning players have success with a modified fan grip. Hold the disc as if you were going to fan your face with it.

Your fingers can either be held against the rim or fanned out, depending on what feels most comfortable. Usually players move fingers in against the rim as they try for more power.

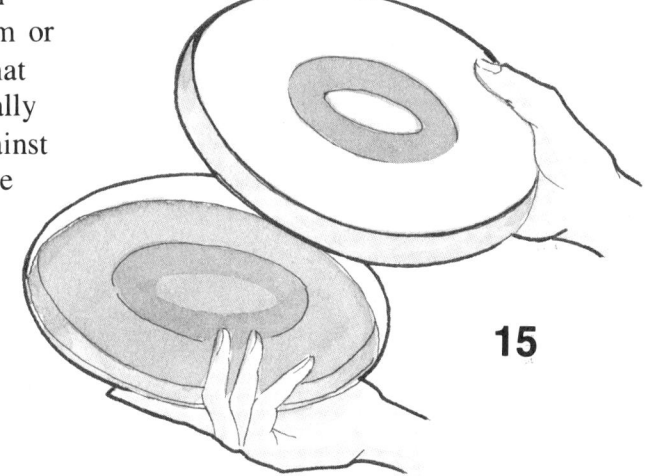

The Stance and Delivery

Don't face the target. Your stance should put your shoulder toward the line of flight.

Start your throwing motion with a backswing that takes the disc and throwing arm across your chest, turning your upper body (A). As your arm moves forward, shift your weight to the lead foot and pull the disc with a straight-arm motion (B). Release with a snap of the wrist and follow through with your upper body and trailing leg (C).

Don't try to throw too hard or far at first. Work at getting smoothness, control, and good spin on the disc. Begin about 10 meters from your partner and work up only as you get smoother releases.

Don't be discouraged if you don't get the results you want right away. Some things take time. If you try too hard, the disc will turn over (right for righties and left for lefties). Concentrate on a smooth snap as if you were snapping a towel. In fact, disc play will definitely make you a better towel snapper.

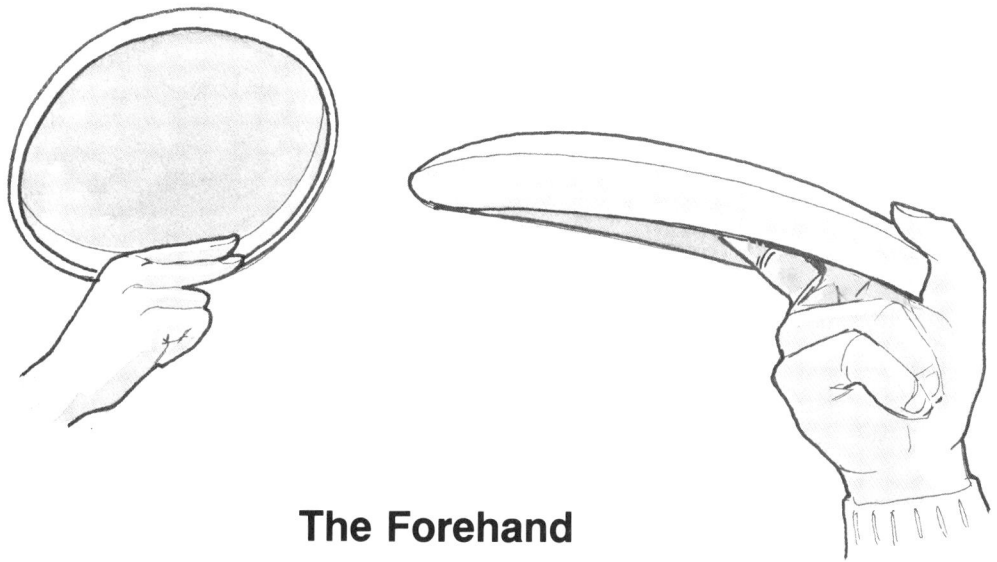

The Forehand

The Grip

In this throw, the two-finger or sidearm grip is used. You must press very firmly with your thumb to control the disc. In this case, you had better not think about the canary example we used for the backhand because a good two-finger grip will kill most canaries.

Imagine you have an eagle by the neck. Make sure your fingers fit comfortably right against the rim and that the disc is at about the angle shown above.

The Stance and Delivery

Again, you stand facing perpendicularly to the line of flight and swing the throwing arm across the front of your body.

Keep the arc of your swing relatively low to keep the flight from turning over. A smooth release is absolutely critical here because the grip provides only a small area of control on the disc. Really concentrate on short, flat flights and work back very gradually.

You will notice that the forehand gives the opposite spin to a backhand flight. Partners not used to it may have trouble catching it at first. You can either be nice and explain it or have the fun of watching them go crazy—your choice.

The Overhand

The Grip

Take your normal backhand grip and simply turn the disc upside down in your hand—you've got it! Let your fingers fan out and squeeze the flight plate between your fingers and thumb.

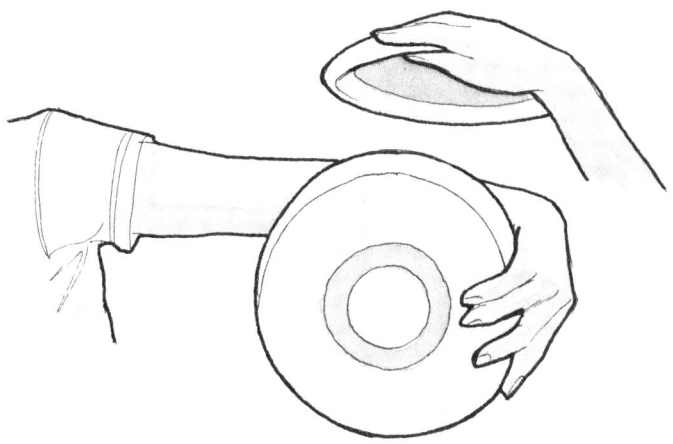

The Stance and Delivery

The overhand probably allows more flexibility in your foot placement than any other shot but generally you will still want to be perpendicular to the line of flight. Start with the disc cocked on top of your forearm for maximum snap. This throw is great fun because it is *much* easier than it looks and you come off like a real pro when you snap one of these away.

Other Variations

We could fill this book with all the ways to put spin on a disc. Here are some hints to get you started (could this be the place that launched a thousand flips?)

1. Swing your backhand lower beside your throwing-side leg—the underhand throw results.
2. Continue the overhand movement around your neck.
3. Release the forehand under either leg or behind your back.
4. Throw your backhand behind your legs.
5. Put your thumb inside the rim and use the forehand motion—the thumber.

. . . And hundreds more!

After It Leaves Your Hand

Curves—Like a little airplane, your Frisbee disc will fly according to its angle in the air. Bank the edge down in the direction you want the disc to curve. Experiment with the height of the curves.

Hover Shots "stall" because the nose of the disc lifts it up and slows the flight. The result is a floater.

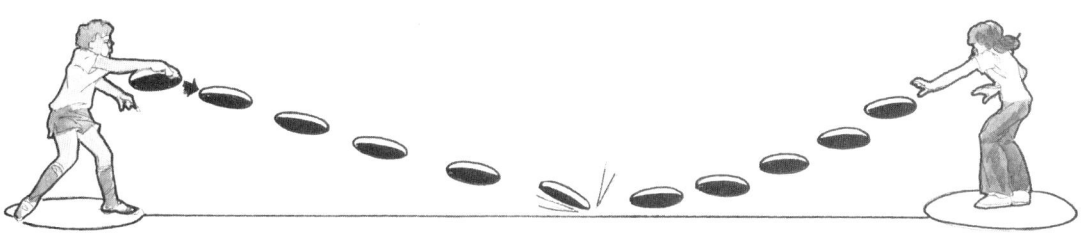

Skips—Start out on a hard playing surface. Later it can be done on grass but a gym floor or concrete is much easier. Throw your backhand so it hits the ground halfway between you and your partner. The cleanest skips will come from low curves—the disc should hit on its edge, not its nose. Left edge for righties—right for lefties. Once you have it working, try the sidearm too. If you can't do this trick, just skip it.

Roller—Rolling the disc can be fun in freestyle, golf and for dogs to chase. You can start with either the sidearm or backhand but you should have the disc hit the ground at least a third of the flight away from you and at about a 45 degree angle to the ground. It will straighten out as it rolls and turn to the topside. You can use this feature to get double curves.

Practicing

Maybe it really isn't practice but you will probably want to get "better" once you start throwing. One way is to do it a lot. Better accuracy comes from really being aware of adjusting your release and learning to deal with the wind. Work for smoothness and lots of spin on the disc. You'll be deadly in no time.

Power and distance come slowly for most people but again, the keys are smoothness and spin. You'll want to add a run-up of five or six steps to your sidearm and backhand delivery to get the most power. It is very important to get a full turn of the body and not to try to get all the power from your arm.

A fun way to work on both distance and accuracy is to play "backoff." Start about 10 steps from your partner and take a step back each time you throw. For a cooperative game, see how many completions you can make without the catcher moving his or her pivot foot. For competition, see who can make the last good throw.

4

CATCHING

If you thought there were a lot of ways to throw a disc, look out because catching has even more possibilities. The first challenge is to be in position to make a catch. Of course a good throw helps but you almost always need to make a few adjustments as the disc flies to you. Really good players never seem to move at all, but that's because they start so early that they don't need to hurry. They can start early because they can read the flight.

Being able to predict where the disc is going to fly is really fun and you will pick up the knack as you play. The trick is to use all the visual information available. By watching the way the disc is thrown and the angle it leaves the thrower's hand, you can begin to know where to move. Of course you're never *absolutely* sure where it's going—that's the fun. If you're into certainty, you should consider shotputting instead.

At first you'll be satisfied to just catch the disc. The pancake catch is a pretty secure start. Just applaud at the right time and you will have made the catch.

After a few of these, the challenge of one-handed catching usually takes over. Remember—the disc is *spinning*. It won't just plop into your hand like a ball. You'll have to *clamp* it. You may have your fingers up or down depending on the height of the catch.

Now the fun really starts. If you can catch with one hand, let's do some trick catches. After all, a one-handed catch is a one-handed catch—right? Start with catching BETWEEN-THE-LEGS. Lift one leg to give yourself more room. Watch the disc right into your hand.

BOTH FEET ON THE GROUND

ONE OFF

NOTHING ON THE GROUND!

Got it? If you're having trouble—get in position a little earlier. It always helps.

The next move is BEHIND-THE-BACK. Turn to the side so you won't have to reach so far. Again, watch the disc into your hand. It takes some practice but soon you will become familiar with the "blind" area behind your back and be catching as easily behind the back as in front of your chest.

Now this one's a bit more exciting. The BEHIND-THE-HEAD catch requires that you reach behind your neck and catch over the shoulder opposite your catching hand. Try this on slow throws first because poor judgment can result in some free plastic surgery.

On high floating shots, go for the ONE FINGER CATCH. Move with the flight of the disc and gently put your finger up under the flight plate. The spin will take your finger to the rim, allowing you to twirl the saucer on your finger.

It's best to practice all of these tricks at the same time rather than working on one at a time. In this way, you don't have to be waiting for a particular kind of throw but can try something on almost any throw. High floater? Try a finger catch.

Low and fast? Do a between-the-legs. Try to trick *every* catch and concentrate on getting into position and deciding on your catch as early as possible.

Here is a trick for one on the ground. Spin it on your finger and pick it up. It's harder than it looks!

5

FLIGHT PLAY

All of the catches in the last chapter have one thing in common. . . Give up? They stop the spin. Well, nothing in this chapter will do that, and in fact, some of the moves *increase* the spin. These are things you can do and still keep the disc flying. Stancil Johnson once wrote that "When a ball dreams, it dreams it's a Frisbee." Well, this is what it is dreaming about.

Tipping

This is the most basic tool of flight play. It consists of keeping the disc aloft by striking the underside of the flight plate. Begin by tipping slow, floating flights with one fingertip. Most players use the middle finger. Tip crisply as near the center of the disc as possible. A helpful aid to staying near the center is to make a small dark dot on the exact middle of the flight plate with a felt pen.

For real control, multiple tips are necessary. This requires adjustment to keep the disc flat. To practice this and some of the other flight play tricks, you should begin to throw the disc up for yourself. This is easy to learn and allows you to practice alone. Hold the disc in both hands in front of your face. "Wind up" by twisting your arms in one direction, crossing your wrists. Now, give the disc a quick, snapping spin. It should rise about a meter and remain flat. Practice will enable you to put a surprising amount of spin on the disc.

Once you have begun to get the feel of finger tipping, you will want to try the elbow, head, knee, toe and heel variations. Each one requires its own special technique but the tipping itself is the same.

TOE

HEEL

HEAD

Perhaps even more useful than tipping is the NAIL DELAY. In a way the nail delay is like a continuous tip. You support the spinning disc with constant contact as it slides on your fingernail. Two things are helpful here: A slippery disc (spray it with silicone and wipe off excess) and good fingernails (this will cure that nail biting).

The finger must be held at a slight angle so that only the nail touches the plastic. Keeping the spinning disc under control takes *lots* of practice. Throw it up for yourself and make small circles with the spin as close to the center of the disc as possible.

Once you can control the delay, you have reached a major plateau in the development of your freestyle play. An unbelieveable number of variations become possible. While some of these are too complex to cover in this book, here are a few to get you started:

—Take the delay on your hand and between your legs or behind your back.

—Delay on one hand and then let the disc roll across that arm, your chest and other arm out to a catch with the other hand.

Once you reach the level of these variations, you will be ready for more advanced reading and play with other hot players who will provide you with the ideas for other combinations. Part of the fun, though, is inventing your own variations using the skills you develop.

—Mix tipping and delaying using both hands, body rolls and spins before catching the disc.

6

FUN AND GAMES

There are as many ways to have fun with a disc as there are players. Almost every group of enthusiasts has developed its own special game or contest. Some of these have become internationally accepted forms of competition while others are still played strictly for fun. Here are the major competitive forms:

FREESTYLE

At some point, you may think, "Hey, we are really hot!" Well . . . if you want to compare yourselves with other folks who feel the same way, competitive freestyle is for you. Teams of two or three get three to five minutes to do their stuff. Usually there is music to play with and other competitors judge the routine on difficulty, variety, execution and presentation. Competitive freestyle can be butterflies time for sure but if you approach it as a positive experience, it can be fun.

MAXIMUM TIME ALOFT

A simple game. Throw the disc up into the wind and catch it on the return flight. Time is measured from the release until the catch which must be made with only one hand. You have to develop a strong throw and learn to use the wind to your advantage to do well.

THROW, RUN & CATCH

A similar event, but the question is how *far* can you throw and still catch the disc? Again, a strong throw and wind knowledge are important but speedy running is a must. Again, you have to catch with one hand—*if* you can get there!

DISTANCE

This one is *really* simple—how far can you throw it?

GOLF

Here is some real fun. It's kind of like ball golf but you don't need clubs. There are a growing number of public courses around the country that are permanently set up with tees and standardized holes that trap the disc when they are hit. Less formal courses use light poles or baskets as the goal objects. Holes usually range from 50 to 150 meters in length and may go around or over such hazards as ponds, trees or buildings. After each throw, the lie for the next shot is where the disc came to rest.

Accurate control, good distance and concentration are the keys to competitive golfing success. You can practice by making up a course around your own neighborhood. Be careful to avoid streets and breakable hazards such as windows. It's often a good idea to make flower beds etc. out of bounds, costing another stroke, to protect them.

DOUBLE DISC COURT

This is our answer to tennis. However, there are always *two* discs in play.

Two players defend each court and attempt to either make the opponents drop a disc or to put both discs in their court at the same time. Good teamwork, flight control and the ability to make a quick catch and release are all important.

FIELD LAYOUT

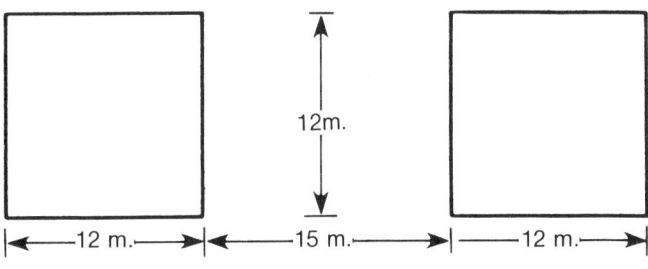

ACCURACY
FIELD TARGET FRONT VIEW

SIDE VIEW

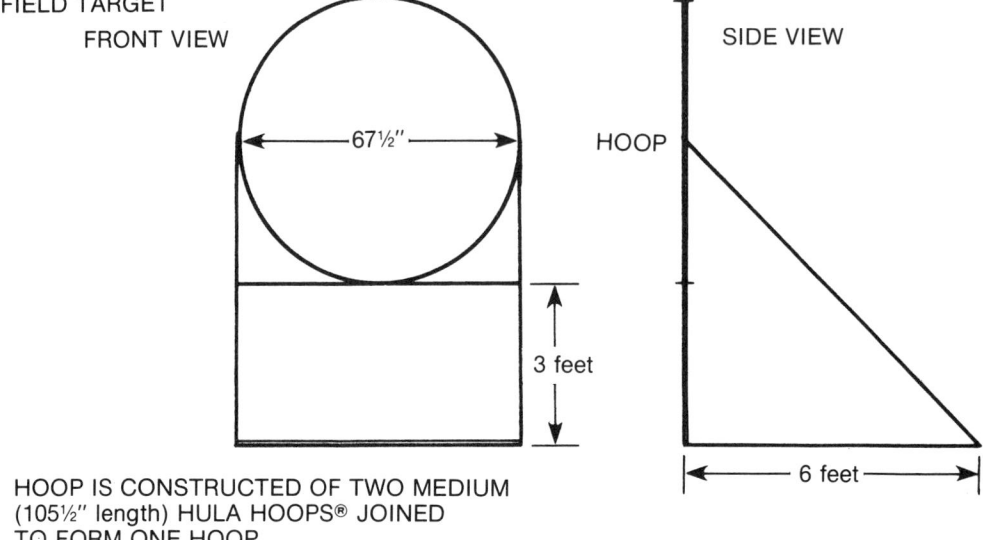

HOOP IS CONSTRUCTED OF TWO MEDIUM (105½" length) HULA HOOPS® JOINED TO FORM ONE HOOP

ACCURACY

A standardized series of 28 throws tells the tale of your accuracy. You get four throws from each site to put the disc through the hoop. It's all concentration.

FIELD LAYOUT

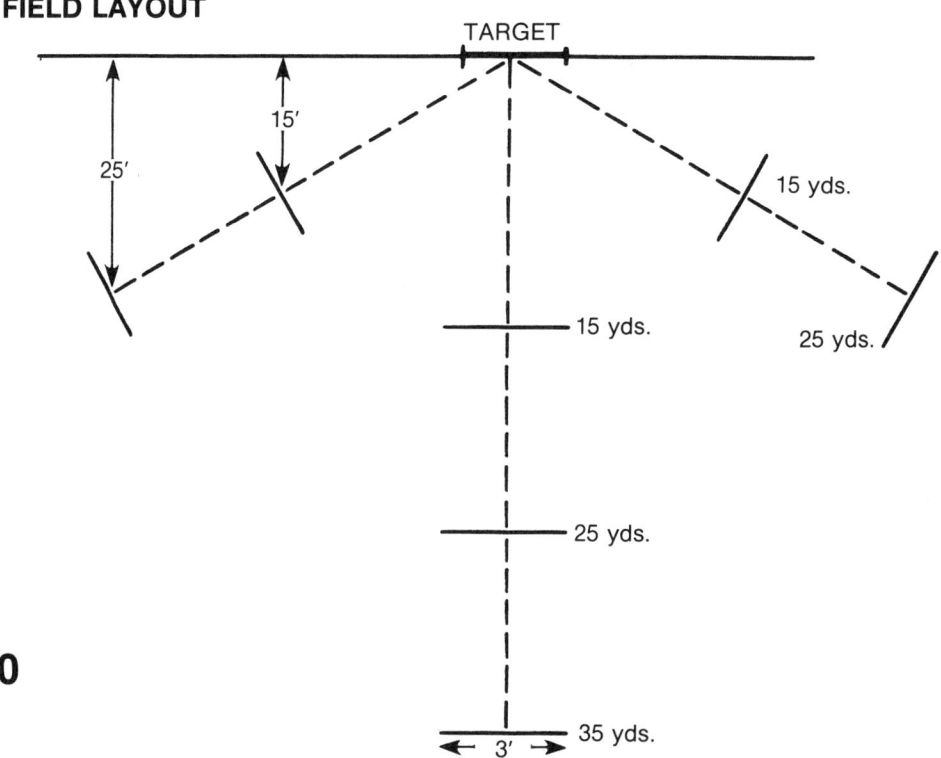

TEAM GAMES
ULTIMATE

Ultimate is a unique team game. The disc is moved down the field from player to player only by passing — no running. When you have the disc, you may only pivot on one foot as in basketball.

Goals are scored by passing to a teammate in the end zone as in a football touchdown pass. In this game though, everyone can be a quarterback *and* a receiver. Defense is man-to-man or zone. Defenders may not touch the offensive players but may knock down or intercept their throws. If they do so, they are immediately on offense. Teamwork is vital but good endurance, solid throwing and speed are needed also.

Many colleges and high schools have Ultimate teams that compete regularly. You will like it.

OFFICIAL ULTIMATE FIELD

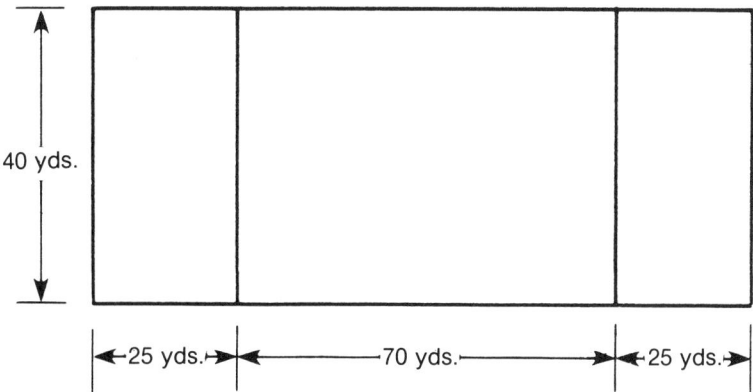

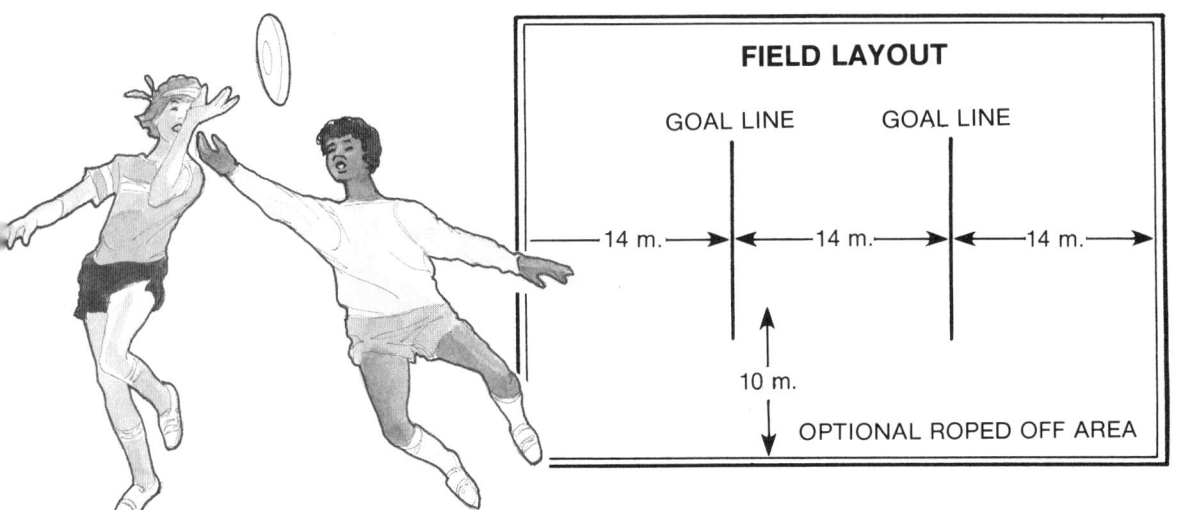

GUTS

Here's the disc game for speed demons. You throw as fast as you can and the other guys try to catch it. That sounds great, but then they throw it back!

The official teams are five per side but three-person teams are often used. Obviously, fast throws and good catching are very important. All the catches must be one-handed, but the team can tip a throw before someone catches it. You will understand the name of this game when you try it.

The Spirit of the Games

Disc sports have historically relied upon the competitors to control themselves. There are no officials in Ultimate or Guts and the players call the plays themselves except in rare cases of honest disagreement in which an official observer is asked to provide a ruling. Players are used to judge freestyle and calls in the field events are made by the competitor. This may seem strange to you but it actually works quite well. We believe it puts the game in a more reasonable perspective. We know the rules and we have agreed to compete under their restrictions. Players take responsibility for themselves rather than trying to violate the rules without being detected by an official. It's a challenge, but a very rewarding opportunity also.

Other Games

Remember that the events we have listed so far are only a small part of what you can do with a disc. There are lots of games you can make up yourself. For instance, instead of the usual freestyle, you can play follow the leader. Each player must attempt the trick done by the leader. Instead of the formal accuracy procedure, you throw at tree trunks or fire hydrants. Fountains make for great accuracy challenges. Loser swims!

Almost any other game adapts well with a few changes and a disc. Try baseball, hockey, football, volleyball and tennis. Even oversized disc croquet works great! And of course, don't forget the pleasures of a throw and catch session. The pace can fit your mood and it's a great excuse for public dancing.

7

PICKING THE RIGHT DISC

So often a new player will ask, "What's the *best* disc?" Because there are so many different disc activities, there can be no single "best" choice. You really must make a selection for each event according to your needs. Your personal requirements relate to your size and strength. If you're just starting out and have small hands, you might try either the 97-gram World Class model or the Premium Fastback. Both have relatively light weight and low rims that are comfortable for smaller hands.

If your strength and size are not a problem, then your selection can relate more to the nature of the event:

Freestyle: The Super Pro and 165-G models are favorites here because of their clean underside flight plate and good stability. The 165-G is quite a handful but it is very "forgiving" because of its large diameter. That is, it has a sweet spot—you can be farther from the center without losing control.

Golf: It's really like picking a club for ball golf. Some players carry 3 or 4 different discs for various types of shots. Basically you want the discs that give you the best combination of distance and control. The World Class models are the most popular.

Maximum Time Aloft/Throw, Run & Catch: The Premium Fastback has become an almost universal choice in these events although heavier winds will occasionally require the 119-G or 110-G models.

Distance: The 119-G and 141-G World Class models have become the popular standard for this event. Your selection depends upon how comfortable you feel with the two sizes.

Accuracy: This is really a matter of taste. It's common to see anything from the Master Tournament model to the Super Pro Frisbee disc.

The team games all have designated discs for each event:
Double Disc Court—110-G
Ultimate—165-G
Guts—Professional Model

As you become more experienced, you will find that you have particular likes and dislikes even between discs of the same model. Especially in the field events and golf, it almost approaches the selection of flies by an avid trout fisherman. Most advanced crazies weigh out each disc to the tenth of a gram to aid in the selection of their throwing stock. It's part of the fun.

8

WHAT'S HAPPENING?

One of the most enjoyable things about any sport or hobby is meeting other enthusiasts and disc play is no exception. In fact our people are so friendly, it is often called the Frisbee disc Family. The biggest organization in the family is the International Frisbee disc Association. There are 125,000 members all over the world. *Frisbee disc World* magazine is published by the I.F.A. six times each year and it reports on all the events, techniques and other items of interest in discdom. There are over 300 clubs in the United States and organizations in 15 foreign countries. Competitions are held at local, state, regional, national and international levels. There is an annual World Junior Frisbee disc Championsip for players 16 years old and younger. World records are also maintained for these age groups by the I.F.A. Here are some of them:

INTERNATIONAL FRISBEE DISC ASSOCIATION
JUNIOR RECORDS

Junior's World Records (13 years - 16 years)

OUTDOOR DISTANCE
388.5 ft. (118.4m)
Scott Zimmerman, Marietta, GA
April 8, 1978 Fredericksburg, VA

INDOOR DISTANCE
252.9 ft. (77.1m)
Scott Zimmerman, Marietta, GA
August 23, 1978 Los Angeles, CA

MAXIMUM TIME ALOFT
10.8 seconds
Krae VanSickle, New York, NY
August 7, 1976 Toronto, Ontario
-and-
10.85 seconds (electronic watch)
Scott Zimmerman, Marietta, GA
August 26, 1978 Los Angeles, CA

THROW, RUN AND CATCH
169.0 ft. (51.5m)
Krae Van Sickle, New York, NY
August 7, 1976 Toronto, Ontario

ACCURACY
17 of 28
Bruce Tashoff, New York, NY
June 25, 1976 New York, NY

MARATHON ULTIMATE
19.5 hours
Varnamo Frisbee disc Club
July 6, 1979 Varnamo, Sweden

GROUP MARATHON
480 hours, 1 minute
Tom and Tina Knisely,
Randy and Kenny McNutt
and Tom Shirey, Canton, OH
Aug 13–Sept 2, 1979, Canton, OH

Children's World Records (12 years -)

OUTDOOR DISTANCE
246.2 ft. (74.8m)
Johnny deLathouder, Birmingham, AL
August 12, 1979 Huntsville, AL

MAXIMUM TIME ALOFT
9.04 seconds
Martel Fein, Philadelphia, PA
September 16, 1978 Ocean City, MD

THROW, RUN AND CATCH
105 ft. (32m)
Scott McGlasson, Monrovia, CA
March 26, 1976 Santa Barbara, CA

ACCURACY
6 of 28
Bobby Stanislaus, Monrovia, CA
April 23, 1977 Irvine, CA

OUTDOOR DISTANCE (under 9 years)
148 ft. (45.1m)
Sandy Frentz, Davis, CA
May 13, 1978 Sonoma, CA

OUTDOOR DISTANCE (under 2 years)
28.5 ft. (8.7m)
Tyler Roddick, Pasadena, CA
Oct. 24, 1979 Pasadena, CA

The I.F.A. also offers proficiency testing on three levels: Expert, Master and World Class Master. Each level requires certain throws and catches.

An increasing number of schools at all levels are beginning to offer disc skill courses in physical education. The I.F.A. has published a course syllabus for use in the teaching of these classes.

For information on any of these activities, write to:
International Frisbee disc Association
P.O. Box 970
San Gabriel, CA   91776

Lifetime membership is $4.00.

So . . . . . HAVE FUN! Remember that these are the *basics*. You should be off to a flying start with what is covered here but there is much more to be learned about what the disc can do and what you can do with it. As you learn, you will discover enough physical and mental challenges to last a lifetime.

It has been said that life is a journey, not a destination. Well, learning to play is the same, so enjoy the flight.

INDEX

Accuracy / 40
Air Speed / 10
Backhand / 15 / 16 / 17
Behind the head catch / 26
Body roll / 33
Clothing / 14
Curves / 10 / 21
Disc selection / 44 / 45
Distance / 37
Double disc court / 39
Exercises / 12 / 13
Forehand / 17 / 18
Frisbee Disc World / 47
Free style / 36
Golf / 38
Guts / 42
Hovering / 21
International Frisbee disc Association / 47
Lift / 10
Maximum time aloft / 36
Morrison, Fred / 8
Nail delay / 32
Officials / 42
One finger catch / 26
Origins / 8
Overhand / 18 / 19
Positioning / 23
Practice / 22
Rolling / 22
Skipping / 21 / 22
Spin / 9
Stability / 10
Stall / 10
Throw, run and catch / 37
Thumber / 20
Tipping / 29 / 30 / 31
Underhand / 20
Ultimate / 41
Wham-O / 9
World records / 46 / 47